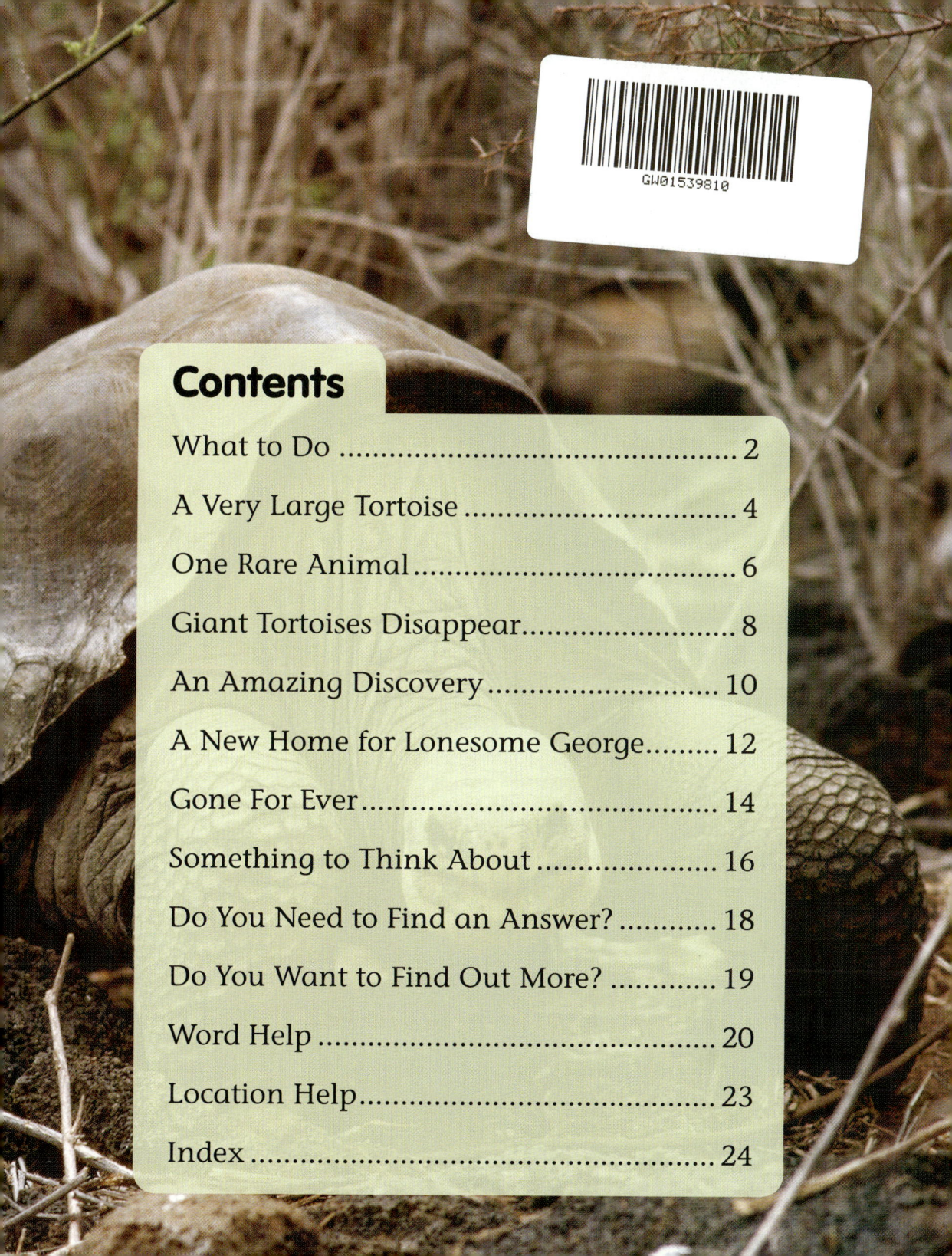

Contents

What to Do 2

A Very Large Tortoise 4

One Rare Animal 6

Giant Tortoises Disappear 8

An Amazing Discovery 10

A New Home for Lonesome George 12

Gone For Ever 14

Something to Think About 16

Do You Need to Find an Answer? 18

Do You Want to Find Out More? 19

Word Help 20

Location Help 23

Index 24

What to Do

Choose a face

Remember the colour you have chosen.

When you see your face on the page, you are the LEADER.

The LEADER reads the text in the speech bubbles.

There are extra words and questions to help you on the teacher's whiteboard. The LEADER reads these aloud.

When you see this stop sign, the LEADER reads it aloud.

STOP
My predictions were right/wrong because . . .

You might need:

- to look at the WORD HELP on pages 20–22;
- to look at the LOCATION HELP on page 23;
- an atlas.

If you are the LEADER, follow these steps:

1 PREDICT

Think about what is on the page.

- Say to your group:

"I am looking at this page and I think it is going to be about . . ."

- Tell your group:

"Read the page to yourselves."

2 CLARIFY

Talk about words and their meaning.

- Say to your group:

"Are there any words you don't know?"

"Is there anything else on the page you didn't understand?"

- Talk about the words and their meanings with your group.
- Read the whiteboard.

- Ask your group to find the LET'S CHECK word in the WORD HELP on pages 20–22. Ask them to read the meaning of the word aloud.

3 ASK QUESTIONS

Talk about how to find out more.

- Say to your group:

"Who has a question about what we have read?"

- Question starters are: how..., why..., when..., where..., what..., who...
- Read the question on the whiteboard and talk about it with your group.

4 SUMMARISE

Think about who and what the story was mainly about.

When you get to pages 16–17, you can talk to a partner or write and draw on your own.

 or

A Very Large Tortoise

Giant tortoises are the biggest tortoises in the world.

A long time ago, many giant tortoises lived on Pinta **Island**.

Most tortoises need their shells to **protect** them. The giant tortoises on Pinta Island didn't need their shells for this. They didn't have **predators**.

I am looking at this page and I think it is going to be about... because...

Are there any words you don't know?

Let's check: predators

Who has a question about what we have read?

What animal do you think could be the predator of a giant tortoise?

These people have come to see some giant tortoises.

This page was mainly about fact fact

STOP My predictions were right/wrong because . . .

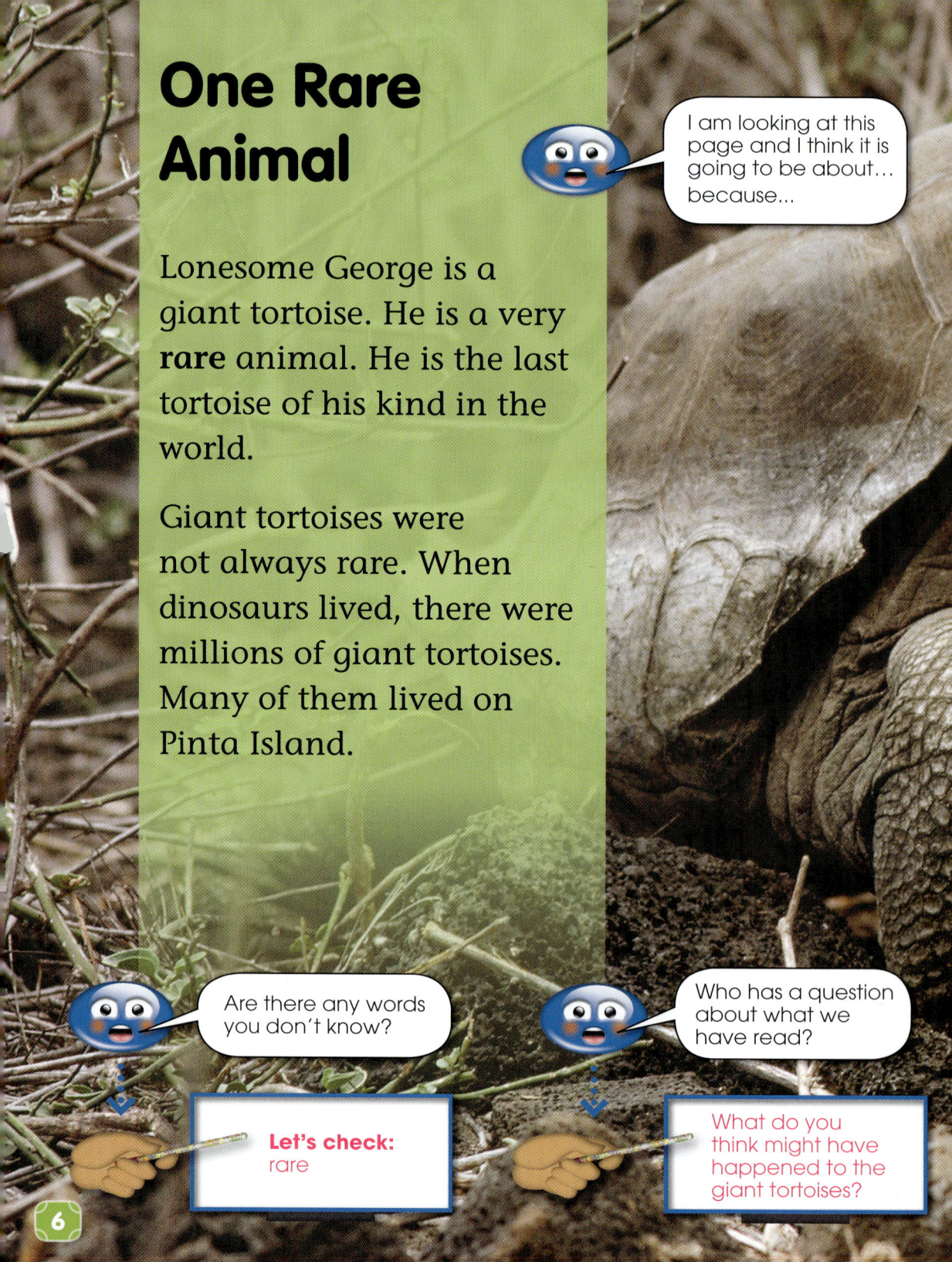

One Rare Animal

I am looking at this page and I think it is going to be about… because…

Lonesome George is a giant tortoise. He is a very **rare** animal. He is the last tortoise of his kind in the world.

Giant tortoises were not always rare. When dinosaurs lived, there were millions of giant tortoises. Many of them lived on Pinta Island.

Are there any words you don't know?

Who has a question about what we have read?

Let's check:
rare

What do you think might have happened to the giant tortoises?

Giant Tortoises Disappear

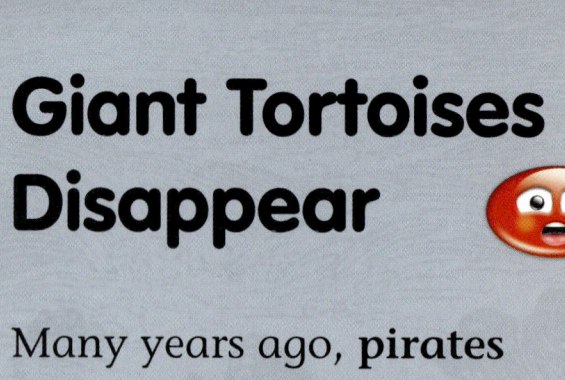

I am looking at this page and I think it is going to be about… because…

Many years ago, **pirates** came to Pinta Island. Giant tortoises were good to eat. They took many away on their ships.

Tortoises can live a long time with little food or water. So they were good food for pirates on long trips.

Soon, there was only one left. This was Lonesome George.

Are there any words you don't know?

Let's check:
drag

Who has a question about what we have read?

Why do you think Lonesome George didn't die too?

Pirates turned the giant tortoises onto their backs. Then, they used ropes to **drag** them to their ship.

This page was mainly about fact fact

STOP My predictions were right/wrong because . . .

An Amazing Discovery

I am looking at this page and I think it is going to be about… because…

It was very exciting to find Lonesome George. He is the only one of his kind in the world. **Scientists** think he could be 70 or 80 years old. This is not really old for a giant tortoise. Some can live to be 200 years old.

Are there any words you don't know?

Who has a question about what we have read?

Let's check: scientists

Do you think Lonesome George will be left on the island? Why?

Giant tortoises live longer than any other animals with a **backbone**.

This page was mainly about fact fact

STOP
My predictions were right/wrong because . . .

A New Home for Lonesome George

Lonesome George couldn't be left on Pinta Island. He was taken to a place where scientists could take care of him. There was a lot of **space** for him in his new home.

Many people come to see Lonesome George. He really looks like an animal that lived with the dinosaurs.

I am looking at this page and I think it is going to be about… because…

Are there any words you don't know?

Who has a question about what we have read?

Let's check:
space

Why do you think Lonesome George couldn't be left on Pinta Island?

Gone For Ever

I am looking at this page and I think it is going to be about… because…

There are many other Giant Tortoises. Some of them are now back on Pinta Island. However, none of them are the same kind as Lonesome George.

When Lonesome George dies, his kind will be **extinct**. They will be gone for ever like the dinosaurs.

Are there any words you don't know?

Let's check:
extinct

Who has a question about what we have read?

What do you think made other animals become extinct?

This baby giant tortoise is being cared for by scientists.

This page was mainly about ... fact fact

STOP
My predictions were right/wrong because . . .

Something to Think About

 or

Think of some important facts and some interesting facts about Lonesome George. Talk about your ideas with a partner, or write them down.

Important Facts

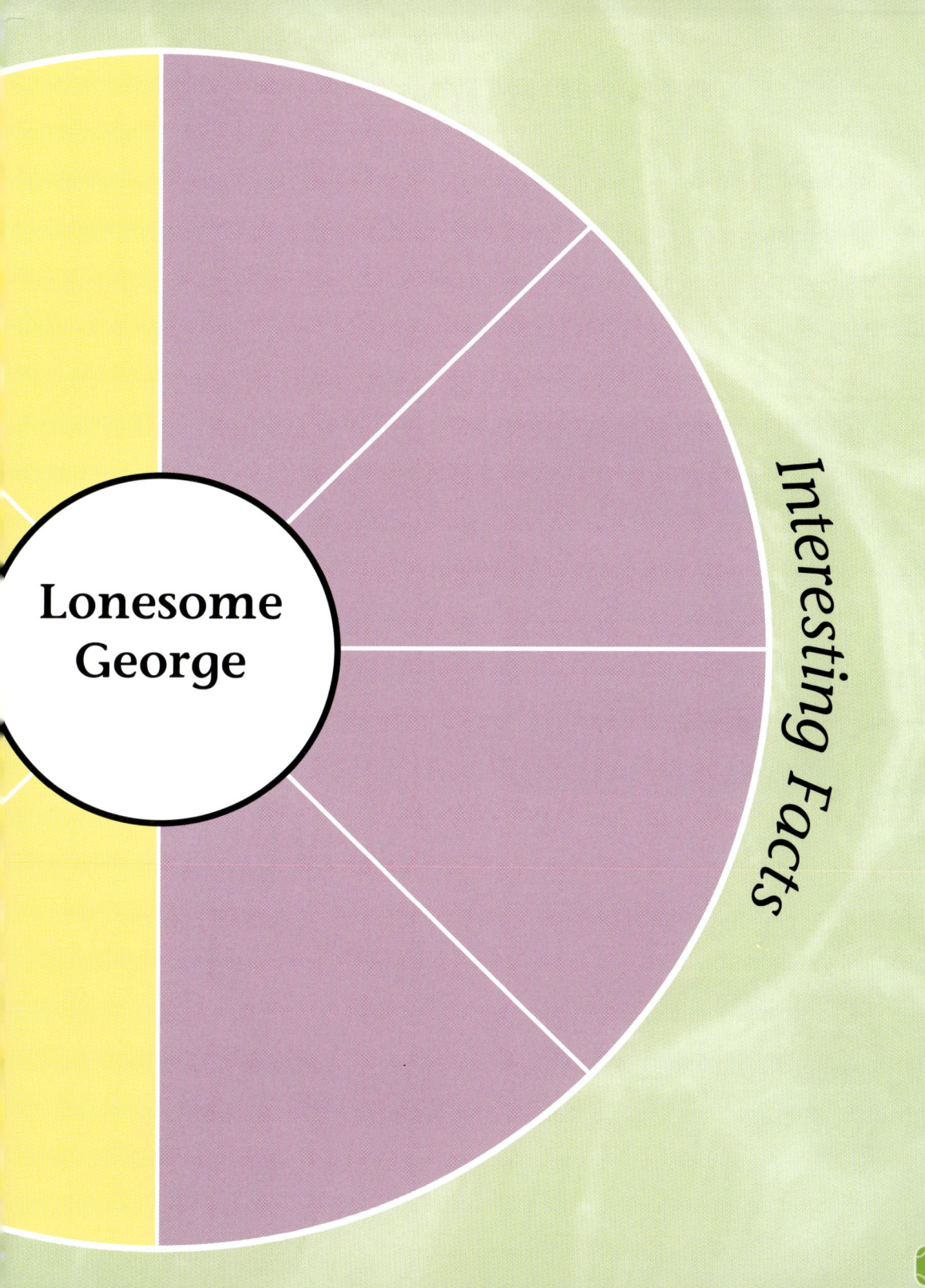

Do You Need to Find an Answer?

You could go to . . .

Library >

Expert >

Internet >

Do You Want to Find Out More?

You could look in books or on the internet. These key words could help you:

extinct animals

giant tortoise

Lonesome George

Pinta Island

Word Help

Dictionary

backbone	bones that are joined or linked in the middle of the back
drag	to pull someone or something along
extinct	no longer living
island	a piece of land with water all around it
pirates	sailors who rob at sea
predators	animals that hunt other animals
protect	to keep something safe from danger
rare	not often found

scientists	people who study or who know a lot about science
space	an open area

Word Help

Thesaurus

drag	pull, tug
extinct	gone for ever, died out
for ever	for always
lonesome	lonely
protection	safety, shelter, shield

Location Help

Where is Pinta Island?

Galapagos Islands

Pinta Island

Index

dinosaurs 6, 12, 14

Lonesome George 6–7, 8, 10, 12–13, 14

Pinta Island 4, 6, 8, 12, 15

pirates 8–9

scientists 10, 12, 15